# Location

## Trip Companions

Trip Duration: _____

Reason For Trip: _____

## What to know before you go

# Notes

## How did it turnout

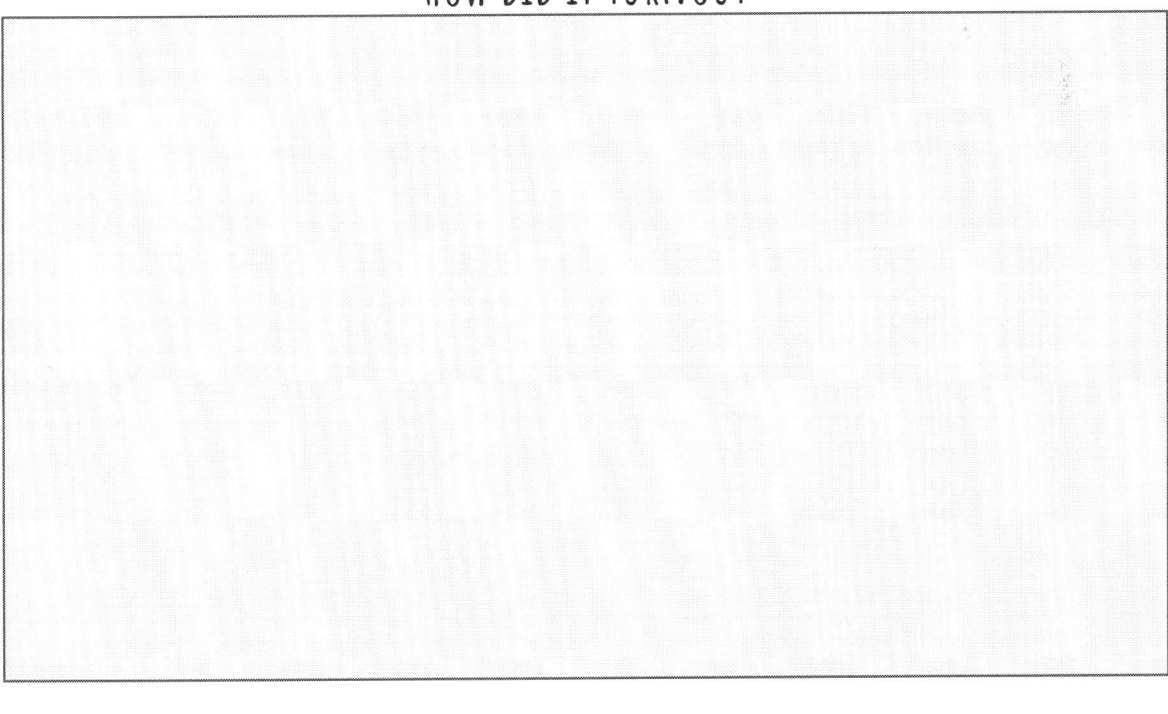

Rating:

## Location

## Trip Companions

_____
_____
_____
_____

Trip Duration: _____

Reason For Trip: _____

## What to know before you go

# NOTES

## HOW DID IT TURNOUT

RATING:

## Location

## Trip Companions

_____
_____
_____
_____

Trip Duration: _____

Reason For Trip: _____

## What to know before you go

# Notes

## How did it turnout

Rating:

## Location

## Trip Companions

_____
_____
_____
_____

Trip Duration: _____

Reason For Trip: _____

## What to know before you go

## NOTES

## HOW DID IT TURNOUT

RATING:

## Location

## Trip Companions

Trip Duration: _____

Reason For Trip: _____

## What to know before you go

# Notes

## How did it turnout

Rating:

## Location

## Trip Companions

_____
_____
_____
_____

Trip Duration: _____

Reason For Trip: _____

## What to know before you go

# Notes

## How did it turnout

Rating:

## Location

## Trip Companions

_____
_____
_____
_____

Trip Duration: _____

Reason For Trip: _____

## What to know before you go

# Notes

## How did it turnout

Rating:

# Location

## Trip Companions

_____
_____
_____
_____

Trip Duration: _____

Reason For Trip: _____

## What to know before you go

## NOTES

_____
_____
_____
_____
_____
_____
_____
_____
_____
_____
_____
_____
_____

## HOW DID IT TURNOUT

RATING:   💩   💩   💩   💩   💩

## Location

## Trip Companions

_____
_____
_____
_____

Trip Duration: _____

Reason For Trip: _____

## What to know before you go

# NOTES

## HOW DID IT TURNOUT

RATING:

## Location

## Trip Companions

Trip Duration: _____

Reason For Trip: _____

## What to know before you go

## Notes

## How did it turnout

RATING:

# Location

# Trip Companions

_____
_____
_____
_____

Trip Duration: _____

Reason For Trip: _____

# What to know before you go

# Notes

## How did it turnout

Rating:

## Location

## Trip Companions

_____
_____
_____
_____

Trip Duration: _____

Reason For Trip: _____

## What to know before you go

# NOTES

## HOW DID IT TURNOUT

RATING:

## Location

## Trip Companions

_____
_____
_____
_____

Trip Duration: _____

Reason For Trip: _____

## What to know before you go

# Notes

## How did it turnout

Rating:

## Location

## Trip Companions

_____
_____
_____
_____

Trip Duration: _____

Reason For Trip: _____

## What to know before you go

# Notes

## How did it turnout

Rating:

## Location

## Trip Companions

_____
_____
_____
_____

Trip Duration: _____

Reason For Trip: _____

## What to know before you go

# NOTES

## HOW DID IT TURNOUT

RATING:

## Location

## Trip Companions

Trip Duration: _____

Reason For Trip: _____

## What to know before you go

# NOTES

## HOW DID IT TURNOUT

RATING:

## Location

## Trip Companions

_____
_____
_____
_____

Trip Duration: _____

Reason For Trip: _____

## What to know before you go

# Notes

## How did it turnout

Rating:

## Location

## Trip Companions

_____
_____
_____
_____

Trip Duration: _____

Reason For Trip: _____

## What to know before you go

# Notes

## How did it turnout

Rating:

## Location

## Trip Companions

_____
_____
_____
_____

Trip Duration: _____

Reason For Trip: _____

## What to know before you go

# Notes

## How did it turnout

Rating:

## Location

## Trip Companions

_____
_____
_____
_____

Trip Duration: _____

Reason For Trip: _____

## What to know before you go

## Notes

_____
_____
_____
_____
_____
_____
_____
_____
_____
_____
_____
_____
_____
_____

## How did it turnout

RATING:

# Location

## Trip Companions

_____
_____
_____
_____

Trip Duration: _____

Reason For Trip: _____

## What to know before you go

## Notes

## How did it turnout

RATING:

# Location

## Trip Companions

_____
_____
_____
_____

Trip Duration: _____

Reason For Trip: _____

## What to know before you go

# Notes

## How did it turnout

Rating:

## Location

## Trip Companions

_____
_____
_____
_____

Trip Duration: _____

Reason For Trip: _____

## What to know before you go

# Notes

## How did it turnout

Rating:

## Location

## Trip Companions

_____
_____
_____
_____

Trip Duration: _____

Reason For Trip: _____

## What to know before you go

## Notes

## How did it turnout

Rating:

## Location

## Trip Companions

Trip Duration: _____

Reason For Trip: _____

## What to know before you go

# NOTES

## HOW DID IT TURNOUT

RATING:

## Location

## Trip Companions

_____
_____
_____
_____

Trip Duration: _____

Reason For Trip: _____

## What to know before you go

## Notes

## How did it turnout

RATING:

# Location

## Trip Companions

_____
_____
_____
_____

Trip Duration: _____

Reason For Trip: _____

## What to know before you go

## Notes

## How did it turnout

RATING:

# Location

## Trip Companions

_____
_____
_____
_____

Trip Duration: _____

Reason For Trip: _____

## What to know before you go

# Notes

## How did it turnout

Rating:

## Location

## Trip Companions

Trip Duration: _____

Reason For Trip: _____

## What to know before you go

# Notes

## How did it turnout

RATING:

## Location

## Trip Companions

Trip Duration: _____

Reason For Trip: _____

## What to know before you go

# Notes

## How did it turnout

Rating:

## Location

## Trip Companions

_____
_____
_____
_____

Trip Duration: _____

Reason For Trip: _____

## What to know before you go

# Notes

---
---
---
---
---
---
---
---
---
---
---
---

## How did it turnout

RATING:

## Location

## Trip Companions

_____
_____
_____
_____

Trip Duration: _____

Reason For Trip: _____

## What to know before you go

# Notes

## How did it turnout

RATING:

## Location

## Trip Companions

_____
_____
_____
_____

Trip Duration: _____

Reason For Trip: _____

## What to know before you go

# Notes

## How did it turnout

Rating:

## Location

## Trip Companions

_____
_____
_____
_____

Trip Duration: _____

Reason For Trip: _____

## What to know before you go

# Notes

## How did it turnout

Rating:

## Location

## Trip Companions

_____
_____
_____
_____

Trip Duration: _____

Reason For Trip: _____

## What to know before you go

# Notes

## How did it turnout

Rating:

## Location

## Trip Companions

_____
_____
_____
_____

Trip Duration: _____

Reason For Trip: _____

## What to know before you go

# Notes

## How did it turnout

RATING:

## Location

## Trip Companions

_____
_____
_____
_____

Trip Duration: _____

Reason For Trip: _____

## What to know before you go

# Notes

## How did it turnout

Rating:

## Location

## Trip Companions

_____
_____
_____
_____

Trip Duration: _____

Reason For Trip: _____

## What to know before you go

# Notes

## How did it turnout

Rating:

## Location

## Trip Companions

_____
_____
_____
_____

Trip Duration: _____

Reason For Trip: _____

## What to know before you go

# Notes

# How did it turnout

RATING:

## Location

## Trip Companions

_____
_____
_____
_____

Trip Duration: _____

Reason For Trip: _____

## What to know before you go

# Notes

## How did it turnout

Rating:

## Location

## Trip Companions

_____
_____
_____
_____

Trip Duration: _____

Reason For Trip: _____

## What to know before you go

# Notes

## How did it turnout

RATING:

## Location

## Trip Companions

_____
_____
_____
_____

Trip Duration: _____

Reason For Trip: _____

## What to know before you go

## Notes

## How did it turnout

RATING:

## Location

## Trip Companions

_____
_____
_____
_____

Trip Duration: _____

Reason For Trip: _____

## What to know before you go

# Notes

## How did it turnout

Rating:

## Location

## Trip Companions

_____
_____
_____
_____

Trip Duration: _____

Reason For Trip: _____

## What to know before you go

# Notes

## How did it turnout

RATING:

## Location

## Trip Companions

_____
_____
_____
_____

Trip Duration: _____

Reason For Trip: _____

## What to know before you go

# Notes

## How did it turnout

Rating:

## Location

## Trip Companions

_____
_____
_____
_____

Trip Duration: _____

Reason For Trip: _____

## What to know before you go

# Notes

## How did it turnout

Rating:

## Location

## Trip Companions

_____
_____
_____
_____

Trip Duration: _____

Reason For Trip: _____

## What to know before you go

## Notes

---

## How did it turnout

Rating:

## Location

## Trip Companions

_____
_____
_____
_____

Trip Duration: _____

Reason For Trip: _____

## What to know before you go

# Notes

## How did it turnout

Rating:

## Location

## Trip Companions

_____
_____
_____
_____

Trip Duration: _____

Reason For Trip: _____

## What to know before you go

# Notes

## How did it turnout

RATING:

## Location

## Trip Companions

_____
_____
_____
_____

Trip Duration: _____

Reason For Trip: _____

## What to know before you go

# Notes

## How did it turnout

Rating:

## Location

## Trip Companions

_____
_____
_____
_____

Trip Duration: _____

Reason For Trip: _____

## What to know before you go

# Notes

## How did it turnout

Rating:

## Location

## Trip Companions

_____
_____
_____
_____

Trip Duration: _____

Reason For Trip: _____

## What to know before you go

# Notes

## How did it turnout

Rating:

## Location

## Trip Companions

_____
_____
_____
_____

Trip Duration: _____

Reason For Trip: _____

## What to know before you go

# Notes

## How did it turnout

RATING:

## Location

## Trip Companions

_____
_____
_____
_____

Trip Duration: _____

Reason For Trip: _____

## What to know before you go

# Notes

## How did it turnout

Rating:

## Location

## Trip Companions

_____
_____
_____
_____

Trip Duration: _____

Reason For Trip: _____

## What to know before you go

# Notes

## How did it turnout

Rating:

## Location

## Trip Companions

_____
_____
_____
_____

Trip Duration: _____

Reason For Trip: _____

## What to know before you go

# Notes

## How did it turnout

Rating:

## Location

## Trip Companions

_____
_____
_____
_____

Trip Duration: _____

Reason For Trip: _____

## What to know before you go

# Notes

## How did it turnout

RATING:

## Location

## Trip Companions

Trip Duration: _____

Reason For Trip: _____

## What to know before you go

# Notes

## How did it turnout

Rating:

## Location

## Trip Companions

_____
_____
_____
_____

Trip Duration: _____

Reason For Trip: _____

## What to know before you go

# Notes

## How did it turnout

Rating:

## Location

## Trip Companions

_____
_____
_____
_____

Trip Duration: _____

Reason For Trip: _____

## What to know before you go

# Notes

## How did it turnout

Rating:

Made in the USA
Middletown, DE
16 June 2023